# Practice Problems in Statistics and Data Reduction

Rahul Basu

Published by Rahul Basu, 2023.

PRACTICE PROBLEMS IN STATISTICS AND DATA REDUCTION

**First edition. July 26, 2023.**



ISBN: 979-8223373537

Written by Rahul Basu.

# Also by Rahul Basu

**CFD methods**
Finite Element Methods

**Standalone**
A Study of the Supply Chain and Financial Parameters of a Small Manufacturing Business
Renewable Energy
Essays on Harvesting of Ocean Energy by Sensor Networks
Ocean and Renewable Energy
Mechanics of Solids
Phase Transformations in Porous Media
Robotics and Automation
Finite Element Methods
Thermodynamics and Heat Engines
Practice Problems in Statistics and Data Reduction

# Table of Contents

To my Parents

# Practice Problems in Statistics and Data Reduction

Rahul Basu

# Problem Set 1

Round Tree Manor is a hotel that provides two types of rooms with three rental classes: Super Saver, Deluxe, and Business. The profit per night for each type of room and rental class is as follows:

| | | Rental Class | | |
|---|---|---|---|---|
| | | **Super Saver** | **Deluxe** | **Business** |
| Room | Type I | $35 | $40 | - |
| | Type II | $15 | $25 | $35 |

Type I rooms do not have wireless Internet access and are not available for the Business rental class. Round Tree's management makes a forecast of the demand by rental class for each night in the future. A linear programming model developed to maximize profit is used to determine how many reservations to accept for each rental class. The demand forecast for a particular night is 140 rentals in the Super Saver class, 65 rentals in the Deluxe class, and 40 rentals in the Business class. Round Tree has 100 Type I rooms and 120 Type II rooms.

(a) Use linear programming to determine how many reservations to accept in each rental class and how the reservations should be allocated to room types.

| Rental Class with room type | No of Reservations |
|---|---|
| Super Saver rentals allocated to room type I | |
| Super Saver rentals allocated to room type II | |
| Deluxe rentals allocated to room type I | |
| Deluxe rentals allocated to room type II | |
| Business rentals allocated to room type II | |

Demand by - Select your answer -Deluxe Super Saver Business Item 6 rental class was not satisfied.

Explain.

The input in the box below will not be graded, but may be reviewed and considered by your instructor.

**(b)** How many reservations can be accommodated in each rental class?

| Rental Class | No of Reservations |
|---|---|
| Super Saver I | ____________________ |
| Deluxe | ____________________ |
| Business | ____________________ |

(c) Management is considering offering a free breakfast to anyone upgrading from a Super Saver reservation to Deluxe class. If the cost of the breakfast to Round Tree is $5, should this incentive be offered?

- Select your answer –Yes or no

Explain.

The input in the box below will not be graded, but may be reviewed and considered by your instructor.

(d) With a little work, an unused office area could be converted to a rental room. If the conversion cost is the same for both types of rooms, would you recommend converting the office to a Type I or a Type II room?

| | Type I | Type II |
|---|---|---|
| Shadow Price | $ | $ |

Convert an unused office area to - Select your answer -Type IType IIItem 15 room.

Explain.

The input in the box below will not be graded, but may be reviewed and considered by your instructor.

(e) Could the linear programming model be modified to plan for the allocation of rental demand for the next night?

- Select your answer –(yes or no) 17

What information would be needed and how would the model change? Explain.

The input in the box below will not be graded, but may be reviewed and considered by your instructor.

# Problem 1.1

Vollmer Manufacturing makes three components for sale to refrigeration companies. The components are processed on two machines: a shaper and a grinder. The times (in minutes) required on each machine are as follows:

**Machine**

| **Component** | **Shaper** | **Grinder** |
|---|---|---|
| 1 | 6 | 4 |
| 2 | 4 | 5 |
| 3 | 4 | 2 |

The shaper is available for 120 hours, and the grinder is available for 110 hours. No more than 200 units of component 3 can be sold, but up to 1000 units of each of the other components can be sold. In fact, the company already has orders for 600 units of component 1 that must be satisfied. The profit contributions for components 1, 2, and 3 are \$8, \$6, and \$9, respectively.

(**a**) Formulate and solve for the recommended production quantities.

Let $C_1$ = units of component 1 manufactured

$C_2$ = units of component 2 manufactured

$C_3$ = units of component 3 manufactured

Max $C_1$ + $C_2$ + $C_3$

s.t.

____ $C_1$ + ____ $C_2$ + ______ $C_3$ - Select your answer -≤≥=Item 7 Shaper

____ $C_1$ + ______ $C_2$ + ______ $C_3$ - Select your answer -≤≥=Item 12 Grinder

__________ $C_3$ - Select your answer -≤≥=Item 15 Maximum units of component 3

________ $C_1$ - Select your answer -≤≥=Item 18 Maximum units of component 1

____________ $C_2$ - Select your answer -≤≥=Item 21 Maximum units of component 2

_______ $C_1$ - Select your answer -≤≥=Item 24 Minimum units of component 1

$C_1$, $C_2$, $C_3$ - Select your answer -≤≥=Item 26 0

Optimal solution: $C_1$, = ______ , $C_2$, = ________ , $C_3$= ___________

(**b**) What are the objective coefficients ranges for the three components?

**Variable Objective Coefficient Range**

$C_1$ - Select your answer -No Lower Limit7.335.466.00Item 30 to - Select your answer -No Upper Limit9.008.569.50Item 31

$C_2$ - Select your answer -No Lower Limit4.335.336.00Item 32 to - Select your answer -No Upper Limit9.008.5610.00Item 33

$C_3$ - Select your answer -No Lower Limit5.005.506.00Item 34 to - Select your answer -No Upper Limit10.009.509.00Item 35

Interpret these ranges for company management.

The input in the box below will not be graded, but may be reviewed and considered by your instructor.

(**c**) What are the right-hand-side ranges?

**Constraint Right-Hand-Side Range**

1 - Select your answer -No Lower Limit430044004500Item 37 to - Select your answer -No Upper Limit744075007550Item 38

2 - Select your answer -No Lower Limit433053306300Item 39 to - Select your answer -No Upper Limit850072006600Item 40

Interpret these ranges for company management.

The input in the box below will not be graded, but may be reviewed and considered by your instructor.

(**d**) If more time could be made available on the grinder, how much would it be worth?

- Select your answer -Profit of $1000Profit of $200NothingItem 42

Explain.

The input in the box below will not be graded, but may be reviewed and considered by your instructor.

(**e**) If more units of component 3 can be sold by reducing the sales price by $4, should the company reduce the price?

- Select your answer –Yes or no)

Explain.

The input in the box below will not be graded, but may be reviewed and considered by your instructor.

# Problem 1.2

The Chamber of Commerce periodically sponsors public service seminars and programs. Currently, promotional plans are under way for this year's program. Advertising alternatives include television, radio, and newspaper. Audience estimates, costs, and maximum media usage limitations are as shown:

| Constraint | Television | Radio | Newspaper |
|---|---|---|---|
| Audience per advertisement | 110,000 | 18,000 | 30,000 |
| Cost per advertisement | $1,500 | $250 | $500 |
| Maximum media usage | 11 | 21 | 13 |

To ensure a balanced use of advertising media, radio advertisements must not exceed 50% of the total number of advertisements authorized. In addition, television should account for at least 10% of the total number of advertisements authorized.

(a) If the promotional budget is limited to $23,000, how many commercial messages should be run on each medium to maximize total audience contact?

| Advertisement Alternatives | No of commercial messages |
|---|---|
| Television | _______________ |
| Radio | _______________ |
| Newspaper | ________________ |

What is the allocation of the budget among the three media?

| Advertisement Alternatives | Budget ($) |
|---|---|
| Television | $ _____ |
| Radio | $ ______ |
| Newspaper | $ ________ |

What is the total audience reached?

_________________

(b) By how much would audience contact increase if an extra $100 were allocated to the promotional budget?

Increase in audience coverage of approximately ________________

# Problem 1.3

The employee credit union at State University is planning the allocation of funds for the coming year. The credit union makes four types of loans to its members. In addition, the credit union invests in risk-free securities to stabilize income. The various revenue-producing investments together with annual rates of return are as follows:

| **Type of Loan/Investment** | **Annual Rate of Return** (%) |
|---|---|
| Automobile loans | 8 |
| Furniture loans | 10 |
| Other secured loans | 11 |
| Signature loans | 12 |
| Risk-free securities | 9 |

The credit union will have $1.8 million available for investment during the coming year. State laws and credit union policies impose the following restrictions on the composition of the loans and investments:

- Risk-free securities may not exceed 25% of the total funds available for investment.
- Signature loans may not exceed 12% of the funds invested in all loans (automobile, furniture, other secured, and signature loans).
- Furniture loans plus other secured loans may not exceed the automobile loans.
- Other secured loans plus signature loans may not exceed the funds invested in risk-free securities.

How should the $1.8 million be allocated to each of the loan/investment alternatives to maximize total annual return?

| **Type of Loan/Investment** | **Fund Allocation** |
|---|---|
| Automobile loans | $__________ |
| Furniture loans | $__________ |
| Other secured loans | $__________ |
| Signature loans | $__________ |
| Risk-free securities | $___________ |

What is the projected total annual return?

Annual Return = $____________

# Problem 2

The "Hospital Infection" dataset gives characteristics of $n = 58$ hospitals in the eastern and north central areas of the United States. The overall purpose for the dataset is to analyze factors that predict *InfctRsk*, the infection risk for patients staying in the hospital. The infection risk value is the percentage of patients who get an infection while they are hospitalized. The variable *Stay*is the average length of stay (days) for patients at the hospital. Assume that a first-order regression model is appropriate.

(a) Calculate a 95% interval estimate of the mean infection risk for patients staying in hospitals with an average length of stay of 10 days. Interpret your confidence interval.

Regression Equation

| InfctRsk | = | -1.160 + 0.5689 Stay |
|---|---|---|

Settings

| Variable | Setting |
|---|---|
| Stay | 10 |

Prediction

| Fit | SE Fit | 95% CI | 95% PI |
|---|---|---|---|
| 4.52885 | 0.134602 | (4.25921, 4.79849) | (2.45891, 6.59878) |

**We can be 95% confident that that in hospitals in which the average length of stay is 10 days, the mean infection risk is between 4.25921 and 4.79849.**

(b) Mercy Hospital has an average length of stay of 10 days. Predict the infection risk for patients staying in Mercy Hospital by calculating a 95% prediction interval. Interpret your prediction interval.

Settings

| Variable | Setting |
|---|---|
| Stay | 10 |

Prediction

| Fit | SE Fit | 95% CI | 95% PI |
|---|---|---|---|
| 4.52885 | 0.134602 | (4.25921, 4.79849) | (2.45891, 6.59878) |

**We can be 95% confident that for any future hospitals in which the average length of stay is 10 days, the mean infection risk is between 2.45891 and 6.59878.**

(c) Is the prediction interval in part (b) wider than the confidence interval in part (a)? Should it be?

(d) Determine the boundary values of the 95% confidence band for the regression line when *Stayh* = 10. (You'll have to calculate this by hand using the formula from Section 2.6 in the textbook.) Is your-confidence band wider at this point than the confidence interval in part (a)? Should it be?

(e) Test, at 0.05 significance level, whether the mean infection risk E(Y_h), when *Stayh* = 8, is less than 4 percent. Write down the test statistic, decision rule, and your conclusion. *[Hint: Think of how to derive a generic t-statistic, i.e., (estimate – hypothesized value) / standard error, then figure out what each part of this formula is.]*

# Homework 1 Regression

**Instructions**: Use Word to type your answers within this document. Then, save and upload your document to Canvas by the due date. The point distribution is located next to each question. Unauthorized distribution and/or uploading of this document is strictly prohibited.

1. (**4 + 4 + 8+ 3 + 5 = 24 points**) Use the "SMSA" dataset. Researchers at General Motors analyzed data on 56 U.S. Standard Metropolitan Statistical Areas (SMSAs) to study whether air pollution contributes to mortality. These data were obtained from the "Data and Story Library" at lib.stat.cmu.edu/DASL/ (the original data source is the U.S. Department of Labor Statistics). The response variable for analysis is *Mort* = age adjusted mortality per 100,000 population (a mortality rate statistically modified to eliminate the effect of different age distributions in different population groups). The dataset includes predictor variables measuring demographic characteristics of the cities, climate characteristics, and concentrations of the air pollutant nitrous oxide ($NO_x$). In particular, *Edu* is median years of education, *Nwt* is percentage nonwhite, *Jant* is mean January temperature in degrees Fahrenheit, *Rain* is annual rainfall in inches, *Nox* is the natural logarithm of nitrous oxide concentration in parts per billion, *Hum* is relative humidity, and *Inc* is median income in thousands of dollars.

a. Fit the multiple linear regression model, $E(Mort) = \beta_0 + \beta_1 Edu + \beta_2 Nwt + \beta_3 Jant + \beta_4 Rain + \beta_5 Nox + \beta_6 Hum + \beta_7 Inc$. Report the SSE (sum of squared errors) and degrees of freedom (df) for error.

**Regression Analysis: Mort versus Edu, Nwt, Jant, Rain, Nox, Hum, Inc**

**Analysis of Variance**

**Source DF Seq SS Seq MS F-Value P-Value**

**Regression 7 150577 21511.0 17.09 0.000**

**Edu 1 50967 50966.9 40.49 0.000**

**Nwt 1 71771 71771.1 57.02 0.000**

**Jant 1 9385 9384.6 7.46 0.009**

**Rain 1 3168 3168.1 2.52 0.119**

**Nox 1 14754 14754.3 11.72 0.001**

**Hum 1 444 443.6 0.35 0.556**

**Inc 1 88 88.3 0.07 0.792**

**Error 48 60417 1258.7**

**Total 55 210994**

**Model Summary**

**S R-sq R-sq(adj) R-sq(pred)**

**35.4779 71.37% 67.19% 59.72%**

**Coefficients**

**Term Coef SE Coef T-Value P-Value VIF**

**Constant 1006.2 95.1 10.58 0.000**

**Edu -15.35 7.25 -2.12 0.040 1.71**

**Nwt 4.214 0.685 6.15 0.000 1.72**

**Jant -2.150 0.659 -3.26 0.002 1.61**

**Rain 1.624 0.564 2.88 0.006 1.83**

**Nox 18.55 5.51 3.37 0.001 1.56**

**Hum 0.537 0.902 0.60 0.555 1.07**

**Inc -0.35 1.30 -0.26 0.792 1.51**

**Regression Equation**

**Mort = 1006.2 - 15.35 Edu + 4.214 Nwt - 2.150 Jant + 1.624 Rain + 18.55 Nox + 0.537 Hum - 0.35 Inc**

**The SSE is 60417 with df of 48.**

a. Do a general linear *F*-test (using a significance level of 5%) to see whether *Hum* and *Inc* provide significant information about the response, *Mort*, beyond the information provided by the other predictor variables.

[In Minitab, you can find the information for the *F*-statistic either by selecting Sequential sums of squares in the regression options for the model in the previous part or by fitting a reduced model without *Hum* and *Inc*. You'll also need to calculate a *p*-value for the *F*-statistic: select Calc > Probability Distributions > F. . . . Select Cumulative probability and leave the Noncentrality parameter set to 0.0. Next, enter in the respective Numerator degrees of freedom and Denominator degrees of freedom. Finally, enter the *F* value of interest into the box that says Input constant. For the output, we will see the *F* value (given as $x$) and the probability $P(X \leq x)$. The p-value for this problem is $1 - P(X \leq x)$. Make sure you know why!]

## Regression Analysis: Mort versus Edu, Nwt, Jant, Rain, Nox, Hum, Inc

**Analysis of Variance**

**Source DF Seq SS Seq MS F-Value P-Value**

**Regression 7 150577 21511.0 17.09 0.000**

**Edu 1 50967 50966.9 40.49 0.000**

**Nwt 1 71771 71771.1 57.02 0.000**

**Jant 1 9385 9384.6 7.46 0.009**

**Rain 1 3168 3168.1 2.52 0.119**

**Nox 1 14754 14754.3 11.72 0.001**

**Hum 1 444 443.6 0.35 0.556**

**Inc 1 88 88.3 0.07 0.792**

**Error 48 60417 1258.7**

**Total 55 210994**

**Model Summary**

**S R-sq R-sq(adj) R-sq(pred)**

**35.4779 71.37% 67.19% 59.72%**

**Coefficients**

**Term Coef SE Coef T-Value P-Value VIF**

**Constant 1006.2 95.1 10.58 0.000**

**Edu -15.35 7.25 -2.12 0.040 1.71**

**Nwt 4.214 0.685 6.15 0.000 1.72**

**Jant -2.150 0.659 -3.26 0.002 1.61**

**Rain 1.624 0.564 2.88 0.006 1.83**

**Nox 18.55 5.51 3.37 0.001 1.56**

**Hum 0.537 0.902 0.60 0.555 1.07**

**Inc -0.35 1.30 -0.26 0.792 1.51**

**Regression Equation**

**Mort = 1006.2 - 15.35 Edu + 4.214 Nwt - 2.150 Jant + 1.624 Rain + 18.55 Nox + 0.537 Hum**

**- 0.35 Inc**

a. Fit the multiple linear regression model, $E(Mort) = \beta_0 + \beta_1 Edu + \beta_2 Nwt + \beta_3 Jant + \beta_4 Rain + \beta_5 Nox$. Check the LINE model assumptions for this model.

[To do this click Graphs in the Minitab regression dialog box. Then select Histogram of residuals, Normal probability plot of residuals, and Residuals versus fits. Also click in the Residuals versus the variables box and type "Edu-Inc." Finally click the Storage button to save the residuals from the model. The resulting 10 plots can be used as follows:

- Use the Histogram, Normal probability plot, and the Ryan-Joiner test to assess the N condition. [To do the Ryan-Joiner test, do the following:

Stat⇒Basic Statistics ⇒ Normality Test, enter RESI for "variable" and click "Ryan-Joiner" for *Tests for Normality.*]

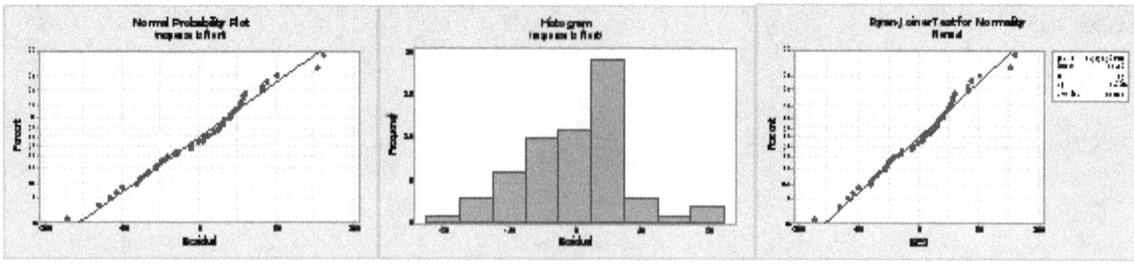

**The Ryan-Joiner test for Normality shows the test statistic is 0.991, which is close to 1 indicating that the errors are normally distributed. The *p*-value is also >.100 which supports the normality.**

- Use the 6 scatterplots of Residuals versus fits and Residuals versus each of the predictors in the model to assess the L, I, and E conditions.

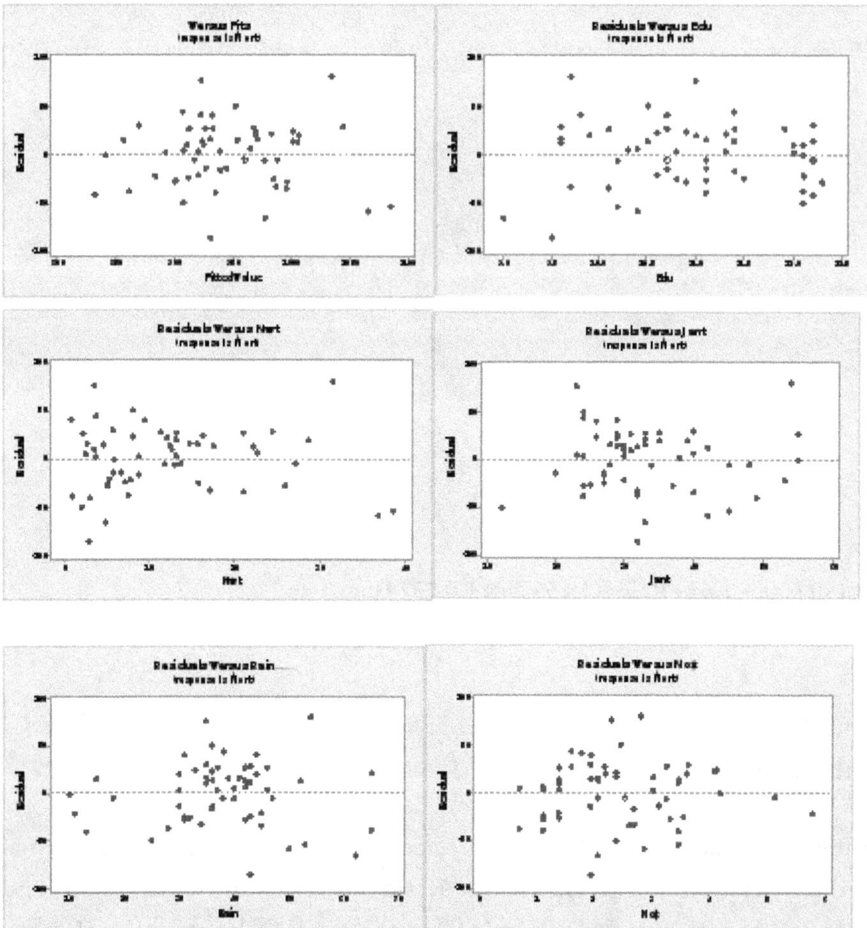

- Use the 2 scatterplots of Residuals versus each of the predictors *not* in the model to assess whether there are systematic patterns to suggest these predictors ought to be in the model.]

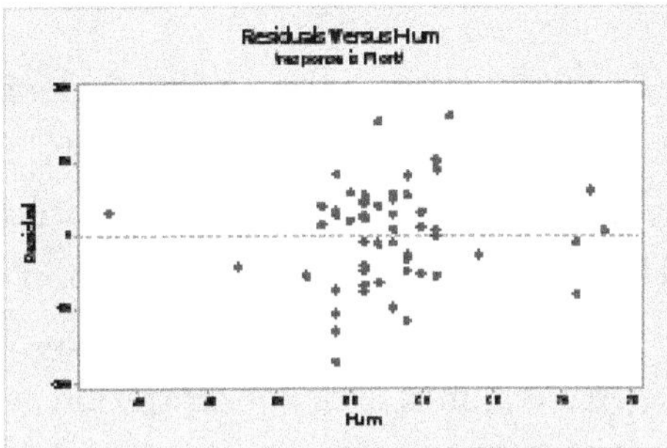


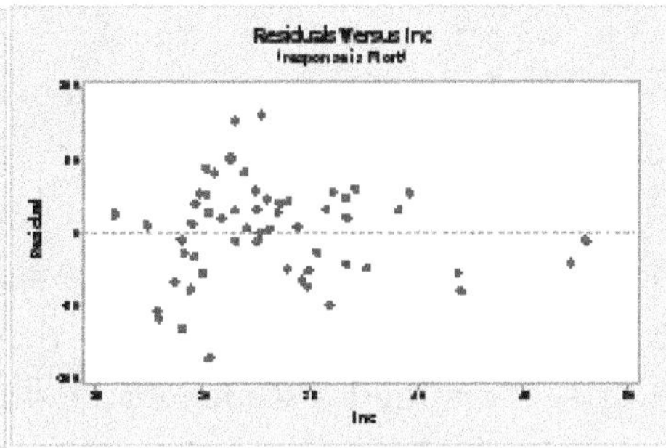


Include all the plots in your write-up and briefly describe the dominant patterns in each plot and your conclusions.

a. Based on the model from part (c), calculate a 95% confidence interval for E*(Mort)* for cities with the following characteristics: *Edu* = 10, *Nwt* = 15, *Jant* = 35, *Rain* = 40, and *Nox* = 2. Interpret your interval.

### Prediction for Mort

**Regression Equation**

**Mort = 1028.2 - 15.59 Edu + 4.181 Nwt - 2.131 Jant + 1.633 Rain + 18.41 Nox**

**Variable Setting**

**Edu 10**

**Nwt 15**

**Jant 35**

**Rain 40**

**Nox 2**

**Fit SE Fit 95% CI 95% PI**

**962.609 8.13329 (946.273, 978.945) (890.605, 1034.61)**

**The 95% confidence interval is (946.273, 978.945). This means that we can be 95% confident that EDU with *Nwt* = 15, *Jant* = 35, *Rain* = 40, and *Nox* = 2 will be between 946.273 and 978.945.**

a. Based on the model from part (c), calculate a 95% prediction interval for *Mort* for a city with the following characteristics: *Edu* = 10, *Nwt* = 15, *Jant* = 35, *Rain* = 40, and *Nox* = 2. Interpret your interval (and say how and why it differs from the interval in the previous part).

**The 95% confidence interval is (890.605, 1034.61). The prediction interval is wider because there is an extra MSE term added to the standard error that the standard error of fit does not have.**

**We can be 95% confident that the EDU with *Nwt* = 15, *Jant* = 35, *Rain* = 40, and *Nox* = 2 will be between 890.605 and 1034.61.**

1. **(5x4=20 points)**Use the dataset "GPA." The director of admissions of a small college selected 120 students at random from the new freshman class in a study to determine whether a student's grade point average (GPA) at the end of the freshman year (Y) can be predicted from the ACT test score ($X_1$). An assistant to the director of admissions conjectured that the predictive power of the model could be improved by adding information on whether the student has chosen a major field of concentration at the time the application was submitted. This is given by $X_2$, that is a dummy variable assuming 1 if student had indicated a major field of concentration at the time of application and 0 if the major field was undecided. Regress Y on $X_1$ and $X_2$.

a. Explain how each regression coefficient in this model is interpreted.

**$Y_i$ = the GPA at the end of the freshman year**

**$x_{i1}$ = the ACT test score**

**$x_{i2}$ = 1 if the student had indicated a major field of concentration at the time of application and**

**$x_{i2}$ = 0 if the major was undecided.**

$$y_i = b_0 + b_1 x_{i1} + b_2 x_{i2} + b_3 x_{i3} + e_i$$

**$\beta_0$ represents the overall average intercept when ignoring group.**

**$\beta_1$ represents the change in mean response for each additional unit increase in the quantitative predictor $x_1$ for both groups.**

**$\beta_2$ represents how far each group is offset from the overall average.**

a. Fit the regression model and state the estimated regression function.

**Regression Analysis: GPA versus ACT, X2**

**Analysis of Variance**

**Source DF Adj SS Adj MS F-Value P-Value**
**Regression 2 4.2927 2.1463 5.57 0.005**
**ACT 1 3.7729 3.7729 9.78 0.002**
**X2 1 0.7048 0.7048 1.83 0.179**
**Error 117 45.1128 0.3856**
**Lack-of-Fit 33 10.5182 0.3187 0.77 0.794**
**Pure Error 84 34.5946 0.4118**
**Total 119 49.4055**

**Model Summary**

**S R-sq R-sq(adj) R-sq(pred)**
**0.620950 8.69% 7.13% 3.58%**

**Coefficients**

**Term Coef SE Coef T-Value P-Value VIF**
**Constant 2.011 0.329 6.12 0.000**
**ACT 0.0399 0.0128 3.13 0.002 1.00**
**X2 0.154 0.114 1.35 0.179 1.00**

## Regression Equation

**GPA = 2.011 + 0.0399 ACT + 0.154 X2**

a. Test whether the X2 variable can be dropped from the regression model; use $\alpha = .01$. State the alternatives, decision rule, and conclusion.

$H_0: b_2 = 0$
$H_A: b_2 \ne 0$

**The test statistic, $t$ = 1.35, has a $p$-value of 0.179 > 0.01 so we fail to reject the null hypothesis and conclude that $\beta 2$ =0. This means that $x2$ does not have a significant linear association with GPA ($y$) and could be dropped from the model.**

a. Conduct a diagnostic analysis for your model and comment on your results.

1. **(5 points)** A marketing research trainee in the national office of a chain of shoe stores used the following response function to study seasonal (winter, spring, summer and fall) effects on sales of a certain line of shoes: $E(Y) = \beta_0 + \beta_1 X_1 + \beta_2 X_2 + \beta_3 X_3$. The Xs are indicator variables defined as follows: $X_1 = 1$ if winter and 0 otherwise; $X_2 = 1$ if spring and 0 otherwise; $X_3 = 1$ if fall and 0 otherwise. After fitting the model, the trainee tested the regression coefficients $\beta_k$ (k=0,1,2,3) and come to the following set of conclusions at an .05 level of significance: $\beta_0 \neq 0$, $\beta_1 = 0$, $\beta_2 \neq 0$ and $\beta_3 \neq 0$. In the report the trainee then wrote: "Results of regression analysis show that climatic and other seasonal factors have no influence in determining sales of this shoe line in the winter. Seasonal influences do exist in the other seasons." Do you agree with this interpretation of the test results? Discuss.

1. **(3x3=9 points)** In a regression study, three types of banks were involved, namely, commercial, mutual savings, and savings and loan. Consider the following system of indicator variables for type of bank:

| **Type of Bank** | X2 | X3 |
|---|---|---|
| Commercial | 1 | 0 |
| Mutual savings | 0 | 1 |
| Savings and loan | 0 | 0 |

a. Develop a first-order linear regression model for relating last year's profit or loss (Y) to size of bank X1 and type of bank (X2, X3).

$$y_i = b_0 + b_1 x_{i1} + b_2 x_{i2} + b_3 x_{i3} + e_i$$

**Where:**
***yi*** **= last year's profit or loss**
***xi*1 = size of the bank**
***xi*2 = type of bank**
***xi*3 = type of bank**

a. State the regression functions for the three types of banks.

**Commercial Bank: *xi*2 = 1 and *xi*3 = 0**

$$\begin{aligned} m_{YC} &= b_0 + b_1 x_{i1} + b_2 x_{i2} + b_3 x_{i3} \\ &= b_0 + b_1 x_{i1} + b_2(1) + b_3(0) \\ &= (b_0 + b_2) + b_1 x_{i1} \end{aligned}$$

$$\backslash\ m_{YC} = (b_0 + b_2) + b_1 x_{i1}$$

**Mutual Savings Bank: *xi*2 = 0 and *xi*3 = 1**

$$\begin{aligned} m_{YMS} &= b_0 + b_1 x_{i1} + b_2 x_{i2} + b_3 x_{i3} \\ &= b_0 + b_1 x_{i1} + b_2(0) + b_3(1) \\ &= (b_0 + b_3) + b_1 x_{i1} \end{aligned}$$

$$\backslash\ m_{YMS} = (b_0 + b_3) + b_1 x_{i1}$$

**Savings & Loan Bank: *xi*2 = 0 and *xi*3 = 0**

$$
\begin{aligned}
m_{y|SL} &= b_0 + b_1 x_{i1} + b_2 x_{i2} + b_3 x_{i3} \\
&= b_0 + b_1 x_{i1} + b_2 (0) + b_3 (0) \\
&= b_0 + b_1 x_{i1}
\end{aligned}
$$

$$\backslash \; m_{y|SL} = b_0 + b_1 x_{i1}$$

a. Interpret the quantities β2 and β3.

**In this case, *β*2 measures the differential effect given by** $m\{y \mid \text{Commercial Bank}\} - m\{y \mid \text{Savings and Loan Bank}\}$

**and *β*2 measures the differential effect given by** $m\{y \mid \text{Mutual Savings Bank}\} - m\{y \mid \text{Savings and Loan Bank}\}$

1. (**4 + 4 + 4 + 4 + 4 + 6 + 4 + 4 + 8 = 42 points**) Use the "Salary" dataset. Three variables in the dataset are *Salary* = annual salary (thousands of U.S. dollars), *YrsExp* = years of work experience, and *Degree* = highest education degree for managers in software companies. The dataset also includes three indicator variables defined as *Deg1* = 1 if highest degree is PhD. and 0 otherwise, *Deg2* = 1 if Master's degree and 0 otherwise, and *Deg3* = 1 if highest degree is Bachelor's degree and 0 otherwise. The sample size is $n$ = 63.

a. Below is a graph of salary versus experience with separate regression lines and symbols for the three different degrees. Discuss the important features of this graph, including whether you think that there may (or may not) be an interaction between degree and years of experience.

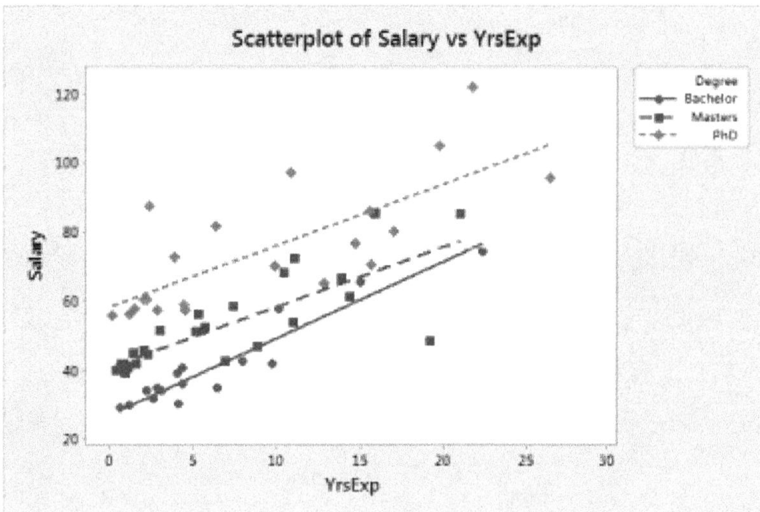


**The regression lines are non-parallel but they do not intersect within the scope of the model. This means that we have an ordinal interaction.**

# HW Problem continued.

a. Fit a simple linear regression model with $y$ = *Salary* and $x$ = *YrsExp*. We will refer to this as the "reduced model" for parts d and e.

**Regression Analysis: Salary versus YrsExp**

**Analysis of Variance**

**Source DF Adj SS Adj MS F-Value P-Value**
**Regression 1 13104.6 13104.6 64.40 0.000**
**YrsExp 1 13104.6 13104.6 64.40 0.000**
**Error 61 12412.8 203.5**
**Lack-of-Fit 60 12161.9 202.7 0.81 0.730**
**Pure Error 1 250.9 250.9**
**Total 62 25517.4**

**Model Summary**

**S R-sq R-sq(adj) R-sq(pred)**
**14.2649 51.36% 50.56% 47.54%**

**Coefficients**

**Term Coef SE Coef T-Value P-Value VIF**
**Constant 40.77 2.70 15.10 0.000**
**YrsExp 2.158 0.269 8.02 0.000 1.00**

**Regression Equation**

**Salary = 40.77 + 2.158 YrsExp**

i. What is the value of the SSE (sum of squared errors) for this regression?

**The SSE is 12412.8.**

i. What is the value of the error df for this regression?

**The error df for this regression is 31.**

a. Fit a multiple linear regression model with $y$ = *Salary* and predictor variables *YrsExp*, *Deg1* and *Deg2*. We will refer to this as the "full model" for parts d and e.

**Regression Analysis: Salary versus YrsExp, Deg1, Deg2**

**Analysis of Variance**

**Source DF Seq SS Seq MS F-Value P-Value**
**Regression 3 20569 6856.3 81.75 0.000**
**YrsExp 1 13105 13104.6 156.25 0.000**
**Deg1 1 6329 6329.4 75.46 0.000**
**Deg2 1 1135 1135.0 13.53 0.001**
**Error 59 4948 83.9**
**Total 62 25517**

**Model Summary**

**S R-sq R-sq(adj) R-sq(pred)**
**9.15815 80.61% 79.62% 77.37%**

**Coefficients**

**Term Coef SE Coef T-Value P-Value VIF**
**Constant 29.27 2.55 11.48 0.000**
**YrsExp 1.841 0.176 10.45 0.000 1.04**
**Deg1 28.36 3.08 9.19 0.000 1.59**
**Deg2 10.71 2.91 3.68 0.001 1.54**

**Regression Equation**

**Salary = 29.27 + 1.841 YrsExp + 28.36 Deg1 + 10.71 Deg2**

i. What is the value of the SSE (sum of squared errors) for this regression?

**The SSE is 4948.**

i. What is the value of the error df for this regression?

**The error df for this regression is 59.**

a. For the model in part c, calculate the value of an *F*-statistic for testing $H_0: \beta_2 = \beta_3 = 0$.

*[Hint: Assume that the variables were entered in the order described in part c. We are testing whether there is any degree effect on mean salary. The null hypothesis is that the coefficients multiplying the degree indicators are both 0. In other words, that there is no degree effect. The regression models that you fit in parts b and c will come into play here. Specifically, the F-statistic for this question is calculated as:*

$$F = \frac{\frac{SSE(reduced) - SSE(full)}{df_E(reduced) - df_E(full)}}{\frac{SSE(full)}{df_E(full)}}$$

*This is what is referred to as a general linear F-statistic.]*

$$F^* = \frac{\frac{SSE(reduced) - SSE(full)}{df_{Error}(reduced) - df_{Error}(full)}}{\frac{SSE(full)}{df_{Error}(full)}} = \frac{\frac{12412.8 - 4948}{31 - 59}}{\frac{4948}{59}} = \frac{7464.8}{-28} \div \frac{4948}{59}$$

$$= \frac{7464.8}{-28} \cdot \frac{59}{4948} = -3.178940986$$

$$\therefore F^* = -3.179$$

a. Refer to the *F*-statistic calculated in part d.

i. What are the df values of this *F*-statistic? *[Hint: The numerator degrees of freedom is given by $df_E(reduced) - df_E(full)$ and the denominator degrees of freedom is given by $df_E(full)$.]*

**The degrees of freedom for the numerator is 28 and the degrees of freedom for the denominator is 59.**

i. What is the *p*-value for the test in part d and what is the appropriate conclusion for the test?

**Cumulative Distribution Function**

**F distribution with 28 DF in numerator and 59 DF in denominator**

**x P( X ≤ x )**

**-3.179 0**

**The *p*-value for this test is 0 <0.001. This means we can reject the null hypothesis. We can state that there is enough evidence to conclude that there is a significant difference in the mean hypothesis for the degrees.**

a. Refer to the regression model you fit in part c (with three predictor variables).

i. Write the estimated sample regression equation.

**Regression Equation**

$$y_i = b_0 + b_1x_{i1} + b_2x_{i2} + b_3x_{i3} + e_i$$

$$\backslash\ m_{Salary} = 29.27 + 1.841YrsExp + 28.36Deg1 + 10.72Deg2$$

i. On the basis of this model, what is the estimated sample regression equation for those with a Bachelor's degree? *[Hint: For a Bachelor's degree person, what are the values of Deg1 and Deg2?]*

**Bachelor's Degree: *Deg*1 = 0 and *Deg*2 = 0**

$$\begin{aligned} m_{Salary|B} &= 29.27 + 1.841YrsExp + 28.36Deg1 + 10.72Deg2 \\ &= 29.27 + 1.841YrsExp + 28.36(0) + 10.72(0) \\ &= 29.27 + 1.841YrsExp \end{aligned}$$

$$\backslash\ m_{Salary|B} = 29.27 + 1.841YrsExp$$

i. On the basis of this model, what is the estimated sample regression equation for those with a Master's degree?

**Master's Degree: *Deg*1 = 0 and *Deg*2 = 1**

$$\begin{aligned} m_{Salary|M} &= 29.27 + 1.841YrsExp + 28.36Deg1 + 10.72Deg2 \\ &= 29.27 + 1.841YrsExp + 28.36(0) + 10.72(1) \\ &= 29.27 + 1.841YrsExp + 10.72 \\ &= 39.99 + 1.841YrsExp \end{aligned}$$

$$\backslash\ m_{Salary|M} = 39.99 + 1.841YrsExp$$

i. On the basis of this model, what is the estimated sample regression equation for those with a PhD. degree?

**Bachelor's Degree: *Deg*1 = 1 and *Deg*2 = 0**

$$\begin{aligned} m_{Salary|PhD} &= 29.27 + 1.841YrsExp + 28.36Deg1 + 10.72Deg2 \\ &= 29.27 + 1.841YrsExp + 28.36(1) + 10.72(0) \\ &= 29.27 + 1.841YrsExp + 28.36 \\ &= 57.63 + 1.841YrsExp \end{aligned}$$

$$\backslash\ m_{Salary|PhD} = 57.63 + 1.841YrsExp$$

a. Refer to the estimated sample regression equation from part f.

i. Write a sentence that interprets the numerical value of the sample regression coefficient that multiplies the variable *Deg1*. *[Hint: Be careful. This coefficient describes the difference between two degree groups.]*

i. Write a sentence that interprets the numerical value of the sample regression coefficient that multiplies the variable *Deg2*.

a. The model you fit in part c allows us to determine mean salary differences between PhD and Bachelor's managers and between Master's and Bachelor's managers. Which indicator variables would you need to include in a regression model that could be used to determine whether there is a significant difference between the mean salaries of Master's and PhD managers? Which estimated regression coefficient would estimate the difference in mean salaries? You don't actually have to estimate your model for this question. *[Hint: Think about how the indicator variable that is left out affects the interpretation of the coefficients for the indicator variables that are included.]*

a. Calculate two interaction variables that are the products, *Deg1*YrsExp* and *Deg2*YrsExp*. These are the variables needed for an interaction model. Carry out a test of whether or not there is a significant interaction between years of experience and highest degree achieved. Describe all details and state a conclusion. *[Hint: To start, fit a multiple regression model that includes the interaction terms as well as the variables from part c. This will be the full model. Think about what is the reduced model.]*

# REGRESSION PROBLEMS CONTD

2.1. Consider the following dataset

| $i$ | 1 | 2 | 3 |
|---|---|---|---|
| $x_i$ | 2 | −6 | 7. |
| $y_i$ | 3 | 4 | 6 |



Fit a regression line using the method of least squares. Determine $r$, $b_1$, and $b_0$.

2.2. **A Perfect Relationship, yet Zero Correlation.** Consider the quadratic relationship $y = x^2$, with data

| $i$ | 1 | 2 | 3 | 4 | 5 |
|---|---|---|---|---|---|
| $x_i$ | −2 | −1 | 0 | 1 | 2. |
| $y_i$ | 4 | 1 | 0 | 1 | 4 |

a. Produce a rough graph for this dataset.
b. Check that the correlation coefficient is $r = 0$.

**2.3. Boundedness of the Correlation Coefficient.** Use the following steps to show that $r$ is bounded by $-1$ and 1 (These steps are due to Koch, 1990).

a. Let $a$ and $c$ be generic constants. Verify

$$0 \leq \frac{1}{n-1}\sum_{i=1}^{n}\left(a\frac{x_i-\overline{x}}{s_x}-c\frac{y_i-\overline{y}}{s_y}\right)^2$$
$$= a^2+c^2-2acr.$$

b. Use the results in part (a) to show $2ac(r-1) \leq (a-c)^2$.
c. By taking $a = c$, use the result in part (b) to show $r \leq 1$.
d. By taking $a = -c$, use the results in part (b) to show $r \geq -1$.
e. Under what conditions is $r = -1$? Under what conditions is $r = 1$?

**2.4. Regression Coefficients Are Weighted Sums.** Show that the intercept term, $b_0$, can be expressed as a weighted sum of the dependent variables. That is, show that $b_0 = \sum_{i=1}^{n} w_{i,0}y_i$. Further, express the weights in terms of the slope weights, $w_i$.

**2.5. Another Expression for the Slope as a Weighted Sum.**

a. Using algebra, establish an alternative expression

$$b_1 = \frac{\sum_{i=1}^{n} weight_i \times slope_i}{\sum_{i=1}^{n} weight_i}.$$

Here, $slope_i$ is the slope between $(x_i, y_i)$ and $(\bar{x}, \bar{y})$. Give a precise form for the weight $weight_i$ as a function of the explanatory variable $x$.

b. Suppose that $\bar{x} = 4$, $\bar{y} = 3$, $x_1 = 2$ and $y_1 = 6$. Determine the slope and weight for the first observation, that is, $slope_1$ and $weight_1$.

2.7. **Regression through the Origin.** Consider the model $y_i = \beta_1 x_i + \varepsilon_i$, that is, regression with one explanatory variable without the intercept term. This model is called *regression through the origin* because the true regression line $\mathrm{E}\, y = \beta_1 x$ passes through the origin (the point (0, 0)). For this model,



the least squares estimate of $\beta_1$ is that number $b_1$ that minimizes the sum of squares $SS(b_1^*) = \sum_{i=1}^{n} (y_i - b_1^* x_i)^2$.

a. Verify that

$$b_1 = \frac{\sum_{i=1}^{n} x_i y_i}{\sum_{i=1}^{n} x_i^2}.$$

b. Consider the model $y_i = \beta_1 z_i^2 + \varepsilon_i$, a quadratic model passing through the origin. Use the result from part (a) to determine the least squares estimate of $\beta_1$.

2.8. a. Show that

$$s_y^2 = \frac{1}{n-1} \sum_{i=1}^{n} (y_i - \bar{y})^2 = \frac{1}{n-1} \left( \sum_{i=1}^{n} y_i^2 - n\bar{y}^2 \right).$$

b. Follow the same steps to show $\sum_{i=1}^{n} (y_i - \bar{y})(x_i - \bar{x}) = \sum_{i=1}^{n} x_i y_i - n\bar{x}\,\bar{y}$.

c. Show that

$$b_1 = \frac{\sum_{i=1}^{n} (y_i - \bar{y})(x_i - \bar{x})}{\sum_{i=1}^{n} (x_i - \bar{x})^2}.$$

d. Establish the commonly used formula

$$b_1 = \frac{\sum_{i=1}^{n} x_i y_i - n\bar{x}\,\bar{y}}{\sum_{i=1}^{n} x_i^2 - n\bar{x}^2}.$$

2.13. **The Correlation Coefficient and the Coefficient of Determination.** Use the following steps to establish a relationship between the coefficient of determination and the correlation coefficient.

a. Show that $\widehat{y}_i - \overline{y} = b_1(x_i - \overline{x})$.

b. Use part (a) to show that $Regress\ SS = \sum_{i=1}^{n} (\widehat{y}_i - \overline{y})^2 = b_1^2 s_x^2 (n-1)$.

c. Use part (b) to establish $R^2 = r^2$.

2.14. Show that the average residual is zero, that is, show that $n^{-1} \sum_{i=1}^{n} e_i = 0$.

2.15. **Correlation between Residuals and Explanatory Variables.** Consider a generic sequence of pairs of numbers $(x_1, y_1), \ldots, (x_n, y_n)$ with the correlation coefficient computed as $r(y, x) = \left[(n-1)s_y s_x\right]^{-1} \sum_{i=1}^{n} (y_i - \overline{y})(x_i - \overline{x})$.

a. Suppose that either $\overline{y} = 0, \overline{x} = 0$ or both $\overline{x}$ and $\overline{y} = 0$. Then, check that $r(y, x) = 0$ implies $\sum_{i=1}^{n} y_i x_i = 0$ and vice versa.

b. Show that the correlation between the residuals and the explanatory variables is zero. Do this by using part (a) of Exercise 2.13 to show that $\sum_{i=1}^{n} x_i e_i = 0$ and then apply part (a).

c. Show that the correlation between the residuals and fitted values is zero. Do this by showing that $\sum_{i=1}^{n} \widehat{y}_i e_i = 0$ and then apply part (a).

Ⓡ EMPIRICAL
*Filename is "AnscombesData"*

**2.19. Summary Statistics Can Hide Important Relationships.** The data in Table 2.9 is due to Anscombe (1973). The purpose of this exercise is to demonstrate how plotting data can reveal important information that is not evident in numerical summary statistics.

a. Compute the averages and standard deviations of each column of data. Check that the averages and standard deviations of each of the $x$ columns are the same, within two decimal places, and similarly for each of the $y$ columns.
b. Run four regressions, (i) $y_1$ on $x_1$, (ii) $y_2$ on $x_1$, (iii) $y_3$ on $x_1$, and (iv) $y_4$ on $x_2$. Verify, for each of the four regressions fits, that $b_0 \approx 3.0$, $b_1 \approx 0.5$, $s \approx 1.237$, and $R^2 \approx 0.677$, within two decimal places.
c. Produce scatter plots for each of the four regression models that you fit in part (b).
d. Discuss the fact that the fitted regression models produced in part (b) imply that the four datasets are similar, though the four scatter plots produced in part (c) yield a dramatically different story.

**Table 2.9**
Anscombe's (1973) Data

| Obs num | $x_1$ | $y_1$ | $y_2$ | $y_3$ | $x_2$ | $y_4$ |
|---|---|---|---|---|---|---|
| 1 | 10 | 8.04 | 9.14 | 7.46 | 8 | 6.58 |
| 2 | 8 | 6.95 | 8.14 | 6.77 | 8 | 5.76 |
| 3 | 13 | 7.58 | 8.74 | 12.74 | 8 | 7.71 |
| 4 | 9 | 8.81 | 8.77 | 7.11 | 8 | 8.84 |
| 5 | 11 | 8.33 | 9.26 | 7.81 | 8 | 8.47 |
| 6 | 14 | 9.96 | 8.10 | 8.84 | 8 | 7.04 |
| 7 | 6 | 7.24 | 6.13 | 6.08 | 8 | 5.25 |
| 8 | 4 | 4.26 | 3.10 | 5.39 | 8 | 5.56 |
| 9 | 12 | 10.84 | 9.13 | 8.15 | 8 | 7.91 |
| 10 | 7 | 4.82 | 7.26 | 6.42 | 8 | 6.89 |
| 11 | 5 | 5.68 | 4.74 | 5.73 | 19 | 12.50 |

# Written Assignment

Complete the following calculation problems and put on word Document or this document.

1. Typical BWR Fuel Rod parameters are as follows:

Table 1: BWR Fuel Rod Parameters

| | |
|---|---|
| Material | Uranium Dioxide |
| Enrichment | .71 to 4.91 w/o* |
| Number of Fuel Pellets | 32,000,000 |
| Total Weight, Uranium | 132.2 metric tons |
| Cladding | Zirconium alloy |
| Cladding Thickness | .03 inches |
| Length of Fuel Rods | 14.66 feet |
| Number of Fuel Rods | 60,356 |
| Fuel Pellet Length | .275 inches |
| Fuel Pellet Diameter | .424 inches |

*w/o is weight percent

Calculate the volume of the fuel based on the parameters given in the table. **(15 points)**

The volume of a cylinder is:

$V=\pi * r^2 * h$ r is the fuel rod radius and h is the fuel rod height.

2. Assume that only $^{235}U$ fissions. Calculate the macroscopic fission cross-section for the fuel given the following parameters: **(20 points)**

(Ignore the trace amounts of $^{234}U$ in the fuel)

| | |
|---|---|
| Density of uranium dioxide | 10.5 $g/cm^3$ |
| w/o of $^{235}U$ in natural uranium | 2.5 w/o (.025) |
| MW of $^{235}U$ | 235.0439 |
| Microscopic fission cross-section of $^{235}U$ | 587 |
| w/o of $^{238}U$ in natural uranium | 99.289 (.99289) |
| MW of $^{238}U$ | 238.0508 |
| Microscopic fission cross-section of $^{238}U$ | ~0 |
| MW of $^{16}O$ | 15.9994 |

3. Calculate the reactor flux given that the required reactor power is 3000MWth. Assume 200MeV/fission. Typical values of the thermal flux in LWRs are on the order of $10^{13}$ at full operating power. **(15 points)**

4. Calculate the moderating ratio for light water at 300°F and at 600°F. Is there a difference?

The parameters in the table are for light water. The cross-sections are at room temperature (68°F). **(25 points)**

$\xi$ .927

$\delta_s$ 103 b

$\delta_a$ .664 b

5. How many collisions are required to slow a neutron from an energy of .5 MeV to a thermal energy of .025 eV using carbon as a moderator? How does this value compare with that tabulated in Table 2 of NP-02, page 27, i.e., why are the values different? For Carbon, $\xi$=.158. (page 27, NP-02)

Note that: "The median fission neutron energy is 1.6 MeV for Pu-239, and the average energy is 2.1 MeV."
http://neutron.kth.se/courses/transmutation/Spectra/Spectra.html. **(25 points)**
Click to download the PDF worksheet of this Written Assignment[1].

1. https://drive.google.com/file/d/0B_CoFMIdBxW3M0o4TjF0N0lwZWs/edit?usp=sharing

# Problem Set Conditional Probability in Decision Trees

In Module Five, our exercise is building on what you have learned in prior modules. The three reference videos for probabilistic top-down tree modeling are provided below. Watch each of these videos as they contain important information that supports the remaining work on the problems as well as the final project:

- Joint Probability Table and Bayes Theorem[1] (14:31)
- Conditional Prob and Joint Prob Table in Excel[2] (6:05)
- Decision Tree with Conditional Probability[3] (22:00)

*Note:* Skip the section on EVSI/EVPI and efficiency; we will do diagnostics later.

**Notes on the videos:** You have already learned everything in the first two videos in prior modules. These videos focus on conditional probability in action. In the third video, Professor Wu uses "marginal probabilities." You may recognize these as weighted probabilities when calculating total probability. However, Wu then uses a slightly different style of calculating a joint probability matrix. While there should be nothing in here that you have not already seen, the reason this is important is that you are going to use these probabilities to construct a tree diagram for decision making. The main take away is that you need to know how to operationalize the story problem into the components for the tree.

**Module Five Problem**: In this problem, you will work through a full decision analysis. The decision includes both a positive branch for determining the business opportunity as well as a negative type branch which evaluates the use of an analyst that may provide unusable results at a cost. It is a great, simple problem to exercise your decision tree skills. Leverage the information from the videos viewed at the beginning of this document as well as your treeplan skills from last module.

**Decision Analysis Problem:** You are a potential business owner in the *hoomaflopper* industry. You have hired Dustin R. Mopps as your industry insider to help you decide which businesses to focus on potentially buying. He has collected useful data from multiple sources for you. The problem with Mr. Mopps is that he is a terrible decision analyst. So, it is up to you to figure out what to do.

Dustin found a business for you to look into for a possible purchase: property ID number 51 in your data set, valued at $188,000. If this property is indeed viable, it is estimated to earn you $500,000 in the first year of business. However, you will have to pay $60,000 to perform a systems audit and refurbish it right after you buy it. Your back-of-the-envelope estimate is that there is **X** chance that you could realize the $500,000. You will need to spend a little time to figure out **X** for your model.

Alternatively, you could hire Dustin to first do some real estate legwork for you, since real estate data is his specialty. He will ask for $16,000 to do further market research for you. From sneakily talking to his other clients, you estimate the probability as 60% that Dustin's market research will be favorable, if the business is going to be **viable**. The probability of an unfavorable report from Dustin is 70% if the business will not be viable. In other words, you trust him, **but not that much**. He might be able to give you an edge. You need to know if it is worth paying him the $16,000 or not. Keep all of these values in mind for your conditional probability calculations.

**Overall Question: What is your optimal strategy for deciding whether to purchase business number 51, based on expected value?**

**Helpful Hints in this Analysis:**

---

1. http://youtu.be/Qcr3ShMDQyc
2. http://youtu.be/5Bc6ZYk6G6k
3. https://www.youtube.com/watch?v=V_pZakI3JMo&feature=youtu.be

- Some thoughts to consider: Do not pay Dustin but just buy it? Walk away from it? Pay Dustin for more research or not? Then buy it on his advice? ...or don't?
- This problem has classic **decision under uncertainty** conditions. A good **decision analysis** should help you answer these questions.
- Consider first that you need to know what **X** is. Without it, you will not be able to proceed.

**Analysis Approach: Following Wu's method, and using the information presented in the problem description, perform the following steps:**

1. You will need to download the following files from Blackboard to the Documents folder
    a. From the Module Five Folder: *Mopps Data Set Data Dictionary* (includes information about the variables)
    b. From DAT 520 Data Files Folder:
        i. *Mopps with Commas*: this is the data set for the problem
        ii. *ProblemSet 5 Tree*: this is the tree we will fill in values to in the exercise
2. Open *Mopps with Commas* in Excel and answer the following questions:
    a. **Question 1:** What is the probability that a property worth at least $150,000 in year 1 ends up worth $200,000 or more in year 5? (**Hint:** Think about numerator and denominator to answer this question. How many properties are there overall? How many properties start out at $150,000+ and then end up at $200,000+ in year 5?)
    b. **Question 2:** What is the probability that a property worth at least $150,000 in year 1 ends up worth more than $279,000 in year 5? (**Hint**: Think about numerator and denominator to answer this question. How many properties are there overall? How many properties start out at $150,000+ and then end up at $279,000+ in year 5?)
3. Open the *ProblemSet 5 Tree* file in Excel
    a. Use the answer for Question 2 above to fill in the X%
    b. Using the information provided with the problem, fill in all of the blue cells on the Excel worksheet.
        i. There are 39 blue cells for 2 points each, totaling 78 points
    c. Calculate the sheet (hit F9)
4. Provide the answers to Question 1 and Question 2 above into Word
5. Further provide the answers to the questions that follow:
    a. Describe and interpret what is going on in this tree in about 250 words.
    b. Include a discussion on what the optimal strategy is and why is it the optimal strategy?
    c. Include a statement of what the *expected value* is? What does expected value mean here?
    d. Change the values in cells B:20 to B:26. These contain the costs and payouts. Change these *one at a time and calculate sheet*. Discuss what threshold values flip the decision tree to recommending a different strategy?
6. Highlight your final tree in Excel, Copy it, and Paste Image at the end of your word document.
7. Save your Word Document and submit via blackboard. Notify your instructor of any issues you encounter.

# Project instructions

**Based on Larson & Farber: sections 5.2–5.3**

Note that you must do this project on your own—you may not work with other students. You are always welcome to ask your instructor for help.

Visit the NASDAQ historical prices weblink[1]. First, set the date range to be for exactly 1 year ending on the Monday that this course started. For example, if the current term started on April 1, 2014, then use April 1, 2013 – March 31, 2014. Next, click the link on the right side of the page that says *Download to Spreadsheet* to save the file to your computer.

This project will only use the Close values. Assume that the closing prices of the stock form a normally distributed data set. This means that you need to use Excel to find the mean and standard deviation. Then, use those numbers and the methods you learned in sections 5.2–5.3 of the course textbook for normal distributions to answer the questions. Do NOT count the number of data points.

Complete this portion of the assignment within a single Excel file. Show your work or explain how you obtained each of your answers. Answers with no work and no explanation will receive no credit.

1. a) Submit a copy of your dataset along with a file that contains your answers to all of the following questions.

   b) What the mean and Standard Deviation (SD) of the Close column in your data set?

   c) If a person bought 1 share of Google stock within the last year, what is the probability that the stock on that day closed at less than the mean for that year? Hint: You do not want to calculate the mean to answer this one. The probability would be the same for any normal distribution. **(5 points)**

1. If a person bought 1 share of Google stock within the last year, what is the probability that the stock on that day closed at more than $750? **(5 points)**
2. If a person bought 1 share of Google stock within the last year, what is the probability that the stock on that day closed within $75 of the mean for that year? **(5 points)**
3. Suppose a person within the last year claimed to have bought Google stock at closing for $650 per share. Would such a price be considered unusual? Use the definition of unusual from the course textbook. **(5 points)**
4. At what prices would Google have to close in order for it to be considered statistically unusual? You will have a low and high value. Use the definition of unusual from the course textbook that is measured as a number of standard deviations. **(5 points)**
5. What are Quartile 1, Quartile 2, and Quartile 3 in this data set? Use Excel to find these values. This is the only question that you must answer without using anything about the normal distribution. **(5 points)**
6. Is the normality assumption that was made at the beginning valid? Why or why not? Hint: Does this distribution have the properties of a normal distribution as described in the course textbook? Real data sets are never perfect, however, it should be close. One option would be to construct a histogram like you did in Project 1 to see if it has the right shape. Something in the range of 10 to 12 classes is a good number. **(5 points)**

There are also **5 points** for miscellaneous items like correct date range, correct mean, correct SD, etc.

---

1. http://www.google.com/finance/historical?q=NASDAQ:GOOG

# THE TRASH BAG CASE

TrashBag Consider the trash bag problem. Suppose that an independent laboratory has tested trash bags and has found that no 30-gallon bags that are currently on the market have a mean breaking strength of 50 pounds or more. On the basis of these results, the producer of the new, improved trash bag feels sure that its 30-gallon bag will be the strongest such bag on the market if the new trash bag's mean breaking strength can be shown to be at least 50 pounds. The mean of the sample of 40 trash bag breaking strengths in Table 1.9 is 50.575. If we let m denote the mean of the breaking strengths of all possible trash bags of the new type and assume that the population standard deviation equals 1.65:

a Calculate 95 percent and 99 percent confidence intervals for m.

b Using the 95 percent confidence interval, can we be 95 percent confident that m is at least 50 pounds? Explain.

c Using the 99 percent confidence interval, can we be 99 percent confident that m is at least 50 pounds? Explain.

d Based on your answers to parts b and c, how convinced are you that the new 30-gallon trash bag is the strongest such bag on the market?

Whole Foods is an all-natural grocery chain that has 50,000 square foot stores, up from the industry average of 34,000 square feet. Sales per square foot of supermarkets average just under $400 per square foot, as reported by USA Today in an article on "A whole new ballgame in grocery shopping." Suppose that sales per square foot in the most recent fiscal year are recorded for a random sample of 10 Whole Foods supermarkets. The data (sales dollars per square foot) are as follows: 854, 858, 801, 892, 849, 807, 894, 863, 829, 815. Using the facts that the sample mean and sample standard deviation are 846.2 and 32.866, respectively,

(1) Find a 95 percent confidence interval for the popu- lation mean sales dollars per square foot for all Whole Foods supermarkets during the most recent fiscal year. Assume normality.

(2) Are we 95 percent confident that this population mean is greater than $800, the historical average for Whole Foods

8.32 Referring to Exercise 8.20 (page 306), regard the sample of 10 sales figures (which has standard deviation 32.866) as a preliminary sample. How large a sample of sales figures is needed to make us 95 percent confident that x, the sample mean sales dollars per square foot, is within a margin of error of $10 of m, the population mean sales dollars per square foot for all Whole Foods supermarkets?

8.37 In each of the following cases, compute 95 percent, 98 percent, and 99 percent confidence intervals for the population proportion p.

a p^�.4 and n�100

c p^�.9 and n�100

b p^�.1 and n�300

d p^�.6 and n�50

# Assignment Case Study

Assignment 1 and 2 is based on the following case study.

**9.6 Case: Cincinnati Veterans Administration Medical Center**

The Cincinnati VA Medical Center (CVAMC) provides health care to eligible veterans in Ohio, southeast Indiana, and northern Kentucky. The CVAMC is an acute care, university affiliated 220-bed facility. It is a part of the Veterans Healthcare Administration of the Department of Veterans Affairs. It comprises one of five medical centers within the Veterans Integrated Services Network 10 (VISN 10). The CVAMC works to provide a variety of services as needed across the continuum of care for veteran patients, as well as trainee education and the pursuit of new knowledge through research. The mission arises from Federal mandates to support health care, education and research.

CVAMC's vision is to "... shape our future by breaking the traditional VA mold, building on our strengths, and emerging as the health care center of choice for all Veterans. As pioneers of change we will:

1. Establish the patient at the core of all processes with the focus on continuity of care leading to optimal patient outcomes.

2. Develop a united team of competent, caring, empowered employees committed to providing service that exceeds expectations.

3. Foster unprecedented labor/management trust and cooperation.

4. Create a proactive organisation that is responsive, streamlined, and personal.

5. Be recognized as an innovative, vital health care leader and educational resource in our VA system and the Greater Cincinnati community."

The CVAMC is able to offer a variety of inpatient and outpatient healthcare services. The Medical Service staff offers services in primary care, general internal medicine, and in multiple medical subspecialties such as cardiology, nephrology, pulmonary, and gastroenterology. The Surgery Service offers general surgical care and specialty care in such areas as urology, orthopedics, vascular surgery and neurosurgery. The Mental Health Service provide.

Psychiatric and psychological support care for patients with a variety of programs including care for patients with post-traumatic stress disorder, substance abuse, and serious mental illnesses. The Neurology Service cares for patients with disorders of the nervous system. It has special programs in epilepsy, neuromuscular disease, stroke, and movement disorders. Physical Medicine and Rehabilitation Service offers support for patients with acute and chronic debilitating conditions. It offers programs in occupational, physical, and speech therapy as well as chronic pain management and prostheses.

The CVAMC also provides specialty services in support of other medical centers within the VISN. This includes surgical, psychiatric, neurological, and medical specialty care to patients at Dayton, Chillicothe, and Columbus. Additionally, some specialized care is offered for veterans from other areas of the state and country, including the production of special limb prostheses.

The primary customer is the veteran patient. Highest priority is given to veterans with medical conditions or injuries related to their service in the military, and to those veterans with limited resources who otherwise would have difficulty obtaining the care they need. CVAMC offers a broad range of services to other eligible veterans as well. Other customers include the families of veteran patients, the veterans support organisations (VSO), the trainees including residents and medical students, and the staff at the other VISN facilities. There is a special relationship with the University of Cincinnati. This involves all three major missions of this medical center. The majority of the staff physicians have joint appointments with the University. Some specialised care is provided through sharing agreements with the University including radiation therapy, special radiological studies, and cardiac surgery. The CVAMC is a major teaching center for many of the University's residents and medical students. The CVAMC also supports researchers with joint appointments at the University. There is a partnership between the unions and the Medical Center. Finally, there is a partnership between the Medical Center and a local elementary school.

The 1,100 employees of the CVAMC include physicians, nurses, psychologists, dieticians, social workers, therapists and other health care professionals. This number also includes those members of the services that support the delivery of care including environmental management, security, medical administration, finance, and acquisition personnel. Physicians represent approximately 10% of the full-time work force, while nursing personnel account for about one-third.

The main facility for the CVAMC includes the acute care bed services and clinic areas housed in one building in Cincinnati. The inpatient facilities include two intensive care units, acute medical and surgical services, and acute and intermediate term psychiatry services. Outpatient facilities include clinics on three floors and a Patient Evaluation Area for patients with emergencies. Full-scale laboratory, clinical pathology, and radiological services are available on-site. There are facilities for computerised fabrication of artificial limbs for patients with amputations. Day treatment facilities are also available for patients with PTSD and substance abuse. The CVAMC operates a nursing home and a domiciliary for homeless veterans at its Fort Thomas location. The CVAMC also supports an outpatient facility in Bellevue, KY for easier access for veteran patients in northern Kentucky. The CVAMC also offers specialty services to other VAMCs in VISN 10 through out reach programs at those facilities. One major regulatory body is the Joint Commission for Accreditation of Healthcare Organisations. Other regulatory bodies that review the activities of the CVAMC include the Nuclear Regulatory Commission, the College of Pathology, The Environmental Protection Agency, and OSHA.

Veteran patients require accessibility to care. This includes the need to be seen at a location convenient to them, as much as possible. Additionally, they must be able to get an appointment with their clinicians within a reasonable period of time. A thirty-day limit for specialty clinic consultation has been targeted as a key customer service standard. Patients do not want to have to wait for long periods on the day of their appointments. They need access to the latest technology and specialty skills as appropriate for their medical conditions. This is important even if the CVAMC does not have the necessary equipment or personnel on site. The CVAMC must then contract for those services. Veteran patients need to have continuity of care. They want to see the same clinician each visit to develop rapport with someone who understands their particular needs. They want that provider to be aware of the results of any specialty consultations or hospitalisations. These patients deserve the availability of a range of services to meet their needs. They recognize the need for interdisciplinary approaches to solve some of their health problems. They demand to be heard during medical decision-making and want their end-of-life wishes respected.

The families of veteran patients need to be informed about the care of their loved ones. They want to be able to participate in educational activities. They wish to be able to support the patient when treatment decisions are being made. They want convenient access to care for the veteran patients, as they are often responsible for getting the patient to the appointments.

The veteran's services organisations play a key role in supporting veteran patients. They demand that the veteran's needs be met. To this end, they require access to top management of the CVAMC in order to discuss their concerns. MBL912L

23

The trainees demand access to teaching facilities. They want to be able to assist in the care of patients with a variety of health conditions. They want to be able to discuss issues with experienced staff. They demand access to the latest technology and treatments. They want to be able to interact with researchers to gain a better understanding of their patients' conditions and options for care.

The staff at other VISN facilities needs to be able to take advantage of the expertise and equipment at the CVAMC when these are not readily available at their own sites. They want access for their patients that is timely and convenient. They demand timely reports of these evaluations and wish to be included in medical decision making.

The University demands satisfaction of its teaching requirements for the trainees. The University requires regular monitoring of the trainees' progress. University staff also monitors the trainees' evaluation of their experience while at the CVAMC. The University requires payment for clinical services provided.

The CVAMC holds a special place in the competitive healthcare market in the region. It is the only hospital in its service area dedicated to veterans. While this limits the number of potential customers, it can use this in its pursuit of its targeted customers. It is relatively small compared to the area's major medical centers, but it can take advantage of its membership in the very large chain of medical centers in the VHA when purchasing medications and equipment. It can also take advantage of its ties with the University and nationally funded research programs to lend an aura of quality. It also provides the most vertically integrated health care delivery system in the market, with a variety of services for its veteran patients across the continuum from outpatient to inpatient. It currently provides care to approximately 21,000 veteran patients, but this represents only about a 10% penetration of its target market. This limited penetration is due in part to years of restricted eligibility to receive care at this facility. Because of its role of supporting veterans with limited resources, it has been viewed at times as a provider of last resort. Federal regulations restrict the ability to advertise, limiting the ability to market its services. The CVAMC also faces a declining population of veterans in its service area.

The CVAMC has a number of competitors in the region. These include all of the major medical facilities which provide inpatient or outpatient care. These compete with the CVAMC mostly for patients with insurance or Medicare coverage. Veteran patients with limited resources may also go to places other than the CVAMC, since some support for indigent care is available. Additionally, the other VA medical centers in the state can compete with the CVAMC for veteran patients. Funding of these centers depends in part on the number of veteran patients served. 24

The CVAMC must be ready to compete with these other facilities, inside and outside of the VHA, if it is to succeed.

There are several factors of importance when competing in this health care market. The reputation for quality may be a critical factor for some patients. Cost is a major factor for many veteran patients, since they have little or no out-of-pocket expenses for care provided at the CVAMC. Accessibility is critical, since patients are often unwilling to tolerate long waits for appointments or long delays on the day of their visits. Many patients show strong preferences for local access to care, the ability to avoid bridge or downtown traffic, and ease of parking. Continuity of care is important to many patients. Many patients want their providers to be able to coordinate their visits and tests, with good communication of results among their providers. Staff courtesy, empathy and efforts to educate the patients may also be factors of importance to health care customers.

Change continues to affect the health care market. Recent changes in federal reimbursement of medical facilities under the Balanced Budget Act have caused financial strain among health care providers. The VHA is funded separately, but is not immune to budget cutting activities in Congress. The insurance companies have also been aggressively trying to reduce their expenses, impacting the revenues of medical facilities. The aging of the population has increased the demand for services. The costs of pharmaceuticals and medical technology continue to rise. Changes in coverage of medications have forced some patients to consider different sources for their healthcare. CVAMC must attend to these changes if it is to prosper in this changing health care environment.

The major new initiative for the CVAMC is to improve access to care by the placement of outpatient facilities at sites more convenient to veteran patients. This process started with the planning for and implementation of the community based outpatient clinic (CBOC) in Bellevue, KY. Analysis of zip code information for eligible veterans in the region showed that there is a high concentration of patients in the three counties of northern Kentucky. Focus groups were held with patients from this area that showed that these patients strongly disliked having to cross the Ohio River for their healthcare. An adequate site was found for a clinic in northern Kentucky. Since its opening, enrollment with patients new to the system has occurred rapidly. In view of this success, the demographic data was reviewed for consideration of two more veterans' service centers. Sites in southeast Indiana and Clermont County have been approved. These should help the CVAMC to meet its targets of increased patient enrollment as well as improved access to care.

The Mental Health Service has undertaken an initiative to improve access to its targeted group of veteran patients in the northern suburbs of Hamilton County. This will also improve access to care and utilization of CVAMC resources as these patients begin to use other services.

The CVAMC has taken part in a new VISN case management program. This involves assigning a nurse to patients in certain high-risk categories. The categories of risk were determined by review of resource utilization including days of hospitalisation. The case manager is trained to improve coordination of care and assure appropriate preventative measures are taken to improve the health state of the patient, limiting the use of scarce resources.

Major research programs are helping the CVAMC achieve its missions. The medical center is one of three sites funded nationally as a Patient Safety Center of Inquiry to look at how mistakes occur and how they can be limited in the delivery of health care. The Mental Health Service has recently received further funding from the National Institutes of Health to study substance abuse management. These programs help to fund staff positions while improving the quality of care that we are able to offer to veteran patients.

The computerized system for automated production of prostheses represents a new service that is not available elsewhere in the VISN. Additionally, it is far superior in cycle time to any system available anywhere else in the region. This system allows the CVAMC to offer its patients with amputations unparalleled service. The shorter cycle time increases the chances that the veteran patient will be able to ambulate well after an amputation procedure. The system allows us to provide similar service for veteran patients at other facilities within the VISN and beyond, without the need for these patients to travel to Cincinnati.

Another area receiving great attention at this time is achieving increasingly strict customer service standards. These help focus attention of all employees on the issues of importance to veteran patients. These standards have associated monitors and measures, with benchmarks from health care systems nationally.

The major unique factor at the CVAMC is the strategic planning process. This occurs at the Quorum, a quarterly meeting of managers from all services as well as representatives of major customer groups. Results of prior initiatives are reviewed. The group decides whether the resources should continue to be assigned to those projects. New initiatives are considered in view of changes in the environment and customer needs. The large size of the group improves organisational buy-in for initiatives. The monitoring activities of this group has allowed the elimination of some committees including the Quality Assurance Committee. The size and nature of this strategic planning group is unusual for a health care organisation. The quarterly 26

meetings allow the medical center to respond more quickly to change. This process will be important in the future success of the CVAMC.

## QUESTIONS

### QUESTION 1

Joe Soap operates a bakery in Durban. Because of the excellent product the bakery produces and its excellent location, demand has increased by 45 % over the previous year. On many occasions, customers were not able to purchase the bread of their choice. Because of the size of the store, no new ovens can be added. At a staff meeting, one employee suggested ways to load the ovens differently so that more loaves of bread can be baked at one time. This new process will improve productivity by 12 % and will require more workers. If they made 2000 loaves of bread the same time last year at a productivity of 2.5 loaves per labour hour, how many more workers will be required? Each worker works 160 hours per month. (10)

**QUESTION 2**

Question 5.14 of prescribed book (page 217) (15)

**QUESTION 3**

The following questions are based on the Cincinnati Veterans Administration Medical Center case study and answers must be relative to the case study.

a) Discuss at least six operational challenges that can prevent CVAMC in meeting the needs of the different types of their customers and the organisation's role in the community and with respect to its competition. (10)

b) Suppose there is a vacancy for an operations manager at CVAMC. What should be a job description of the new operations manager? (10)

c) The Board of CVAMC has decided to follow a low cost leadership strategy. Discuss the content of an operations plan to support this decision (hint – study figure 2.4 of the prescribed book (page 73)). (15)

d) "Quality is about meeting customer requirements." Suggest with full motivation how at least two quality improvement approaches can be used to improve quality at CVAMC.

(15)

e) What will be the advantages and disadvantages of implementing an ISO 9001:2015 standard? (15)

f) Suppose CVAMC is designed with 2000 beds for patients. However the financial director insisted that best optimum cost will be to accommodate only 1500 patients at any given time. Further, due to staffing issues only 1200 patients could be accommodated at any given time. What is the utilisation and efficiency in terms of patient accommodation at any given time? (10)

GET
FILE='C:\Users\Anthony Johnson\Downloads\ECAS(6) (3).sav'.
Warning # 5281. Command name: GET FILE

## SPSS Statistics is running in Unicode encoding mode.

This file is encoded in

a locale-specific (code page) encoding. The defined width of any string variables are automatically tripled in order to avoid possible data loss. You can use ALTER TYPE to set the width of string variables to the width of the longest observed value for each string variable.

```
DATASET NAME DataSet1 WINDOW=FRONT.
REGRESSION
/MISSING LISTWISE
/STATISTICS COEFF OUTS R ANOVA
/CRITERIA=PIN(.05) POUT(.10)
/NOORIGIN
/DEPENDENT hb_r
/METHOD=ENTER age gender.
```

## Regression

**Notes**

| | | |
|---|---|---|
| Output Created | | 15-FEB-2017 19:50:59 |
| Comments | | |
| Input | Data | C:\Users\Anthony Johnson\Downloads\ECAS(6) (3).sav |
| | Active Dataset | DataSet1 |
| | Filter | <none> |
| | Weight | <none> |
| | Split File | <none> |
| | N of Rows in Working Data File | 8774 |
| Missing Value Handling | Definition of Missing | User-defined missing values are treated as missing. |
| | Cases Used | Statistics are based on cases with no missing values for any variable used. |
| Syntax | | REGRESSION<br>/MISSING LISTWISE<br>/STATISTICS COEFF OUTS R ANOVA<br>/CRITERIA=PIN(.05) POUT(.10)<br>/NOORIGIN<br>/DEPENDENT hb_r<br>/METHOD=ENTER age gender. |
| Resources | Processor Time | 00:00:00.03 |
| | Elapsed Time | 00:00:00.03 |
| | Memory Required | 1972 bytes |
| | Additional Memory Required for Residual Plots | 0 bytes |

[DataSet1] C:\Users\Anthony Johnson\Downloads\ECAS(6) (3).sav

**Variables Entered/Removed**[a]

| Model | Variables Entered | Variables Removed | Method |
|---|---|---|---|
| 1 | Gender, Age (years)[b] | . | Enter |

a. Dependent Variable: Haemoglobin (g/dL) enrolment

b. All requested variables entered.

**Model Summary**

| Model | R | R Square | Adjusted R Square | Std. Error of the Estimate |
|---|---|---|---|---|
| 1 | .103[a] | .011 | .010 | 1.63421 |

a. Predictors: (Constant), Gender, Age (years)

**ANOVA[a]**

| Model | | Sum of Squares | df | Mean Square | F | Sig. |
|---|---|---|---|---|---|---|
| | Regression | 218.400 | 2 | 109.200 | 40.889 | .000[b] |
| 1 | Residual | 20368.946 | 7627 | 2.671 | | |
| | Total | 20587.346 | 7629 | | | |

a. Dependent Variable: Haemoglobin (g/dL) enrolment

b. Predictors: (Constant), Gender, Age (years)

**Coefficients[a]**

| Model | | Unstandardized Coefficients | | Standardized Coefficients | t | Sig. |
|---|---|---|---|---|---|---|
| | | B | Std. Error | Beta | | |
| | (Constant) | 13.204 | .128 | | 103.459 | .000 |
| 1 | Age (years) | -.002 | .002 | -.015 | -1.304 | .192 |
| | Gender | -.349 | .039 | -.105 | -9.018 | .000 |

a. Dependent Variable: Haemoglobin (g/dL) enrolment

**Use the following table for Questions 1-4.**

It shows the data for

# 10 sample orders for Bob's sporting goods.

| Customer ID | Gender | Payment Type | Sales Total | Customer Experience Rating (1-5) |
|---|---|---|---|---|
| A1 | Female | Cash | $68.12 | 1 |
| A2 | Female | Credit | $52.27 | 5 |
| A3 | Female | Credit | $85.35 | 1 |
| A4 | Male | Cash | $82.00 | 3 |
| A5 | Male | Debit | $91.00 | 1 |
| A6 | Female | Credit | $60.00 | 4 |
| A7 | Male | Cash | $46.00 | 5 |
| A8 | Female | Credit | $40.00 | 5 |
| A9 | Female | Debit | $25.00 | 3 |
| A10 | Female | Credit | $16.00 | 3 |

1) Customer Experience Rating is a(n)___________variable.

A. Ordinal
B. Interval
C. Nominal
D. Ratio

2) Sales Total is measured as a(n)__________variable.

A. Ratio
B. Nominal
C. Interval
D. Ordinal

3) How many variables are qualitative?

A. 2
B. 3
C. 4
D. 5

4) The Customer Experience Rating was most likely collected through:

A. Experiment
B. Focus Group
C. Survey
D. Direct Observation

**For Questions 5-7, use data from pertinent worksheet in the Excel data file embedded on Page 1 of this exam.** It shows the number of complaints to Billy Bob's Emporium.

5) Using the $2^k > n$ rule, how many classes are required?

A. 3
B. 4
C. 5
D. 6

6) Using class width of 3, set lower and upper bounds for first class to be 2 and 4, respectively. What is the relative frequency of the third class?

A. .2
B. .125
C. .25
D. .025

7) Which histogram accurately depicts the data provided?

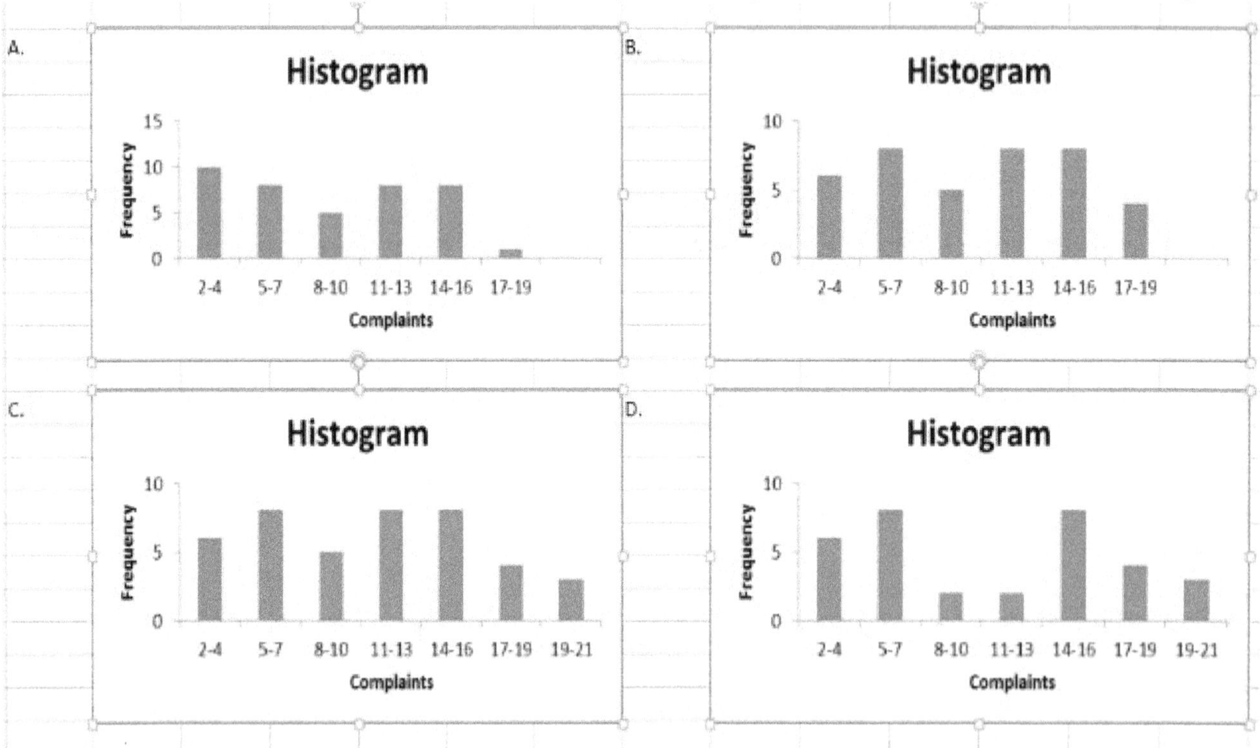


**For Questions 8 - 10, use data from pertinent worksheet in the Excel data file embedded on Page 1 of this exam.** It shows the number of pizzas sold weekly at Pizza Gallery.

8) Which variable is independent?

A. Pizza's sold weekly
B. Week
C. Could be either variable
D. Shown on the vertical axis

9) Which stem and leaf plot is an accurate depiction of the data?

**Stem unit: 100**

A.

| Stem | Leaf |
|---|---|
| 2 | 45666899 |
| 3 | 02356899 |
| 4 | 000001123444555666777 89 |
| 5 | 11456667799999 |

B.

| Stem | Leaf |
|---|---|
| 3 | 33345666899 |
| 4 | 02356899 |
| 5 | 00000112344455566677789 |
| 6 | 11456667799999 |

C.

| Stem | Leaf |
|---|---|
| 2 | 33345666899 |
| 3 | 02356899 |
| 4 | 00000112 |
| 5 | 11456667799999 |

D.

| Stem | Leaf |
|---|---|
| 2 | 33345666899 |
| 3 | 02356899 |
| 4 | 00000112344455566677789 |
| 5 | 11456667799999 |

10) Which scatter plot accurately describes the data provided?

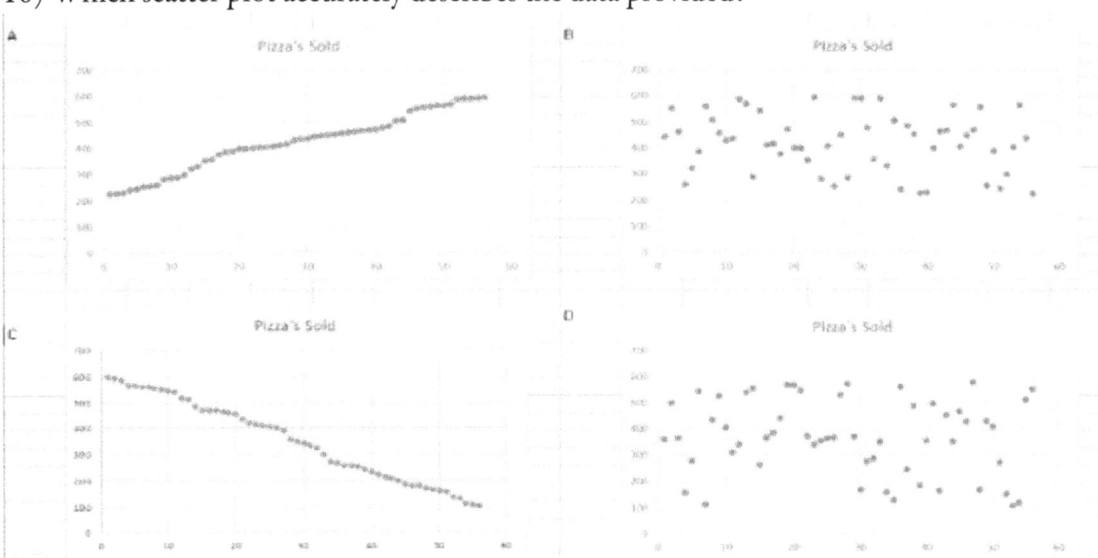


**For Questions 11 – 19, use data from pertinent worksheet in the Excel data file embedded on Page 1 of this exam.** It is data for car sales at a dealership.

11) The mode for the number of sales people is

A. 5
B. 13
C. 17
D. Both B and C are correct

12) The average number of new cars sold is

A. 9.98
B. 5.35
C. 11.45
D. 8.82

13) Which of the following statements is true

A. New cars sold has a st dev of 3.66 and is more dispersed (less consistent) than Used cars sold
B. New cars sold has a st dev of 3.66 and is less dispersed (more consistent) than Used cars sold
C. New cars sold has a st dev of 13.41 and is more dispersed (less consistent) than Used cars sold
D. New cars sold has a st dev of 13.41 and is less dispersed (more consistent) than Used cars sold

14) The median for Used Cars sold is

A. 3.75
B. 7
C. 6
D. 13

15) The range for profit from Used car sales is

A. $42,156
B. $68,588
C. $20,958
D. $23,200

16) Use Excel's function to compute the 35$^{th}$ percentile for profit from New car sales?

A. $30,049
B. $46,235
C. $28,200
D. 14

17) For number of Used cars sold, which of the following are true?

A. Store A1 is an outlier
B. There are no outliers
C. Stores A1, A9, A11, A15 and A22 are outliers
D. Stores A2, A5 and A32 are outliers

18) The mode for the BBB rating is?

A. 15
B. AAA
C. 10
D. AA and AA+

19) Use Excel's function to compute interquartile range for sales people.

A. 6.15
B. 15.00
C. 13.20
D. 7.25

20) Bison football fans making the 18 hour drive from Fargo ND to Frisco TX purchased gasoline 6 times (see table below). What is the average price they paid per gallon of gas?

| Purchase | Gallons Purchased | Price Paid/Gallon |
|---|---|---|
| 1 | 15 | $1.90 |
| 2 | 8 | $2.31 |
| 3 | 22 | $1.87 |
| 4 | 5 | $2.85 |
| 5 | 16 | $1.99 |
| 6 | 14 | $2.05 |

A. $2.16 per gallon
B. $2.04 per gallon
C. $1.87 per gallon
D. $1.99 per gallon

**Use the following information to answer questions 21-23.**

500 employees of your company are listed by age and their score on computer proficiency test:

**Test Scores**

| Age | *150<* | *150-169* | *170-199* | *≥200* | **Total** |
|---|---|---|---|---|---|
| 20-29 | 10 | 25 | 30 | 65 | **130** |
| 30-39 | 10 | 20 | 55 | 45 | **130** |
| 40-49 | 15 | 20 | 60 | 25 | **120** |
| 50-59 | 5 | 10 | 45 | 25 | **85** |
| ≥60 | 5 | 5 | 10 | 15 | **35** |
| **Total** | **45** | **80** | **200** | **175** | **500** |

21) What is the probability that a randomly selected employee is in 40-49 years age range and scores 170 or more?

A. 0.353
B. 0.17
C. 0.708
D. 0.754

22) What is the probability that a randomly selected employee scores 170 or more and is 50 years or older?

A. 0.19
B. 0.253
C. 0.412
D. 0.44

23) One of the employees scored in range of 200 or higher. What is the probability this employee is younger than 40?

A. 0.22
B. 0.371
C. 0.629
D. 0.722

**Use the following information to answer questions 24-25:**

Chance of winning $100 or more on a type of casino slot machine is 2.3%, when playing the maximum bet for one hour. A couple enters the casino and each plays these machines for an hour.

24) What is the chance that both win $100 or more?

A. 0.0005
B. 0.0046
C. 0.046
D. 0.023

25) What is the chance that one of them wins $100 or more?

A. 0.046
B. 0.023
C. 0.0225
D. 0.0449

26) What is the probability that neither of them win $100 or more?

A. 0.4561
B. 0.9700
C. 0.9545
D. 0.9980

**Use the following information to answer questions 27 and 28:**

Eight balls are in a basket: white, black, blue, green, yellow, red, orange, and violet. You will draw 3 balls from the basket without replacement. After drawing each ball you will not return it to the basket, until all 3 balls are drawn. Then you will return all balls to the basket for the next draw of 3.

27) What is the probability that you will draw the white, yellow, and red balls – in that order – in the first draw of 3 balls?

A. 0.029
B. 0.0030
C. 0.0004
D. 0.0021

28) What is the probability that the white and the red balls are, respectively, the first and second balls drawn on the first draw of 3 balls, and again the first and second balls drawn on the second draw of 3 balls?

A. 0.0022
B. 0.0001
C. 0.0003
D. 0.0178

**Use this information to answer questions 29 and 30:**

You and your nine friends (a group of 10) are planning for a day of activity. Six of you will play basketball with another team while four will stand by. In the evening the entire group will go to a concert and enjoy your favorite music.

29) Assuming everybody in your group can play but only 6 of you will be in the team, how many different basketball teams can you form? Note: A different team means at least one player is different.

A. 5040
B. 3604
C. 860
D. 210

30) In how many different ways can your group line up at the ticket booth of the concert? Assume single file.

A. Less than or equal to 100,000 different ways
B. More than 100,000 but less than or equal to 1,000,000 different ways
C. More than 1,000,000 but less than or equal to 2,000,000 different ways
D. More than 2000,000 different ways

31) Historical data shows that 0.65% of finished products (65 in 10,000) from of a production line is faulty and must be either refurbished or scrapped. You are inspecting a box of 100 units from the latest production batch. What is the probability that you will find one faulty unit? Use Excel to solve. Assume Binomial distribution.

A. 0.28
B. 0.34
C. 0.65
D. 0.06

32) Cars arrive at a gas station at an average rate of 5 per minute. What is the probability that 8 cars arrive at this gas station within the next minute? Assume Poisson distribution.

A. 0.28
B. 0.34
C. 0.65
D. 0.06

**Use this information to answer questions 33-34:**

The following probability distribution summarizes sales statistics for a new product for 50 business days:

| #Units sold during the day | Frequency (days) |
|---|---|
| 1 | 3 |
| 2 | 5 |
| 3 | 4 |
| 4 | 8 |
| 5 | 2 |
| 6 | 8 |
| 7 | 7 |
| 8 | 6 |
| 9 | 5 |
| 10 | 2 |
| **Total** | **50** |

33) What is the expected number of units sold per day?

A. Less than 4
B. 4 or more, but less than 5

C. 5 or more, but less than 6
D. More than 6

34) What is the variance of daily sales?

A. 82.51
B. 2.54
C. 5.44
D. 6.45

35) Your business plan indicates that the new product line may turn in $68,000 profit next year if demand is strong, $24,000 profit if demand is average and $15,000 loss if demand is weak. Market study shows 35% probability for a strong demand, 40% probability for average demand, and 25% for a weak demand next year. What is the expected monetary value (EMV) of this new product line for next year?

A. $29,650
B. $31,440
C. $39,286
D. $41,223

36) A management professor gives a quiz containing 15 True/False questions. Past data suggests the probability to be 0.78 that a student chooses the correct answer for any given question. What is the probability that a student selected at random will answer at least 12 questions correctly? Assume binomial distribution applies.

A. 0.2457
B. 0.3269
C. 0.5726
D. 0.6731

37) The probability that an article in XYZ magazine has a typographical error is 0.05. The next edition has 18 articles. What is the probability that the magazine (all 18 articles) will be free of typographical errors? Assume binomial distribution.

A. 0
B. 0.3972
C. 0.95
D. 1.00

**Use the following information to answer Questions 38 – 40.**
Students arrive at the reference desk of the library at an average rate of 12 per hour. Assume Poisson distribution applies.

38) Compute the probability that exactly 5 students arrive in one hour.

A. 0.0127
B. 0.0034
C. 0.0203
D. 0.1606

39) Compute the probability that exactly 5 students arrive in 30 minutes.

A. 0.0127
B. 0.0034
C. 0.0203
D. 0.1606

40) Compute the probability that **at least 15** students arrive in the next two hours.

A. 0.0724
B. 0.9802
C. 0.0344
D. 0.8444

**Use the following information to answer Questions 41-42.**
The time it takes to make a kitchen cabinet is uniformly distributed and ranges between 125 to 200 minutes.

41) What is the probability that it takes exactly 180 minutes to make a kitchen cabinet?

A. 0
B. 0.3329
C. 0.7333
D. 1.2861

42) What is the probability that it takes between 150 to 220 minutes to make a kitchen cabinet?

A. 0.5
B. 0.3759
C. 0.6667
D. 0.9333

**Use the following information to answer Questions 43 – 45.**
The mean time it takes for a particular make/model of a watch to break down and require repair services from the manufacturer is 30 months, with a standard deviation of 8 months. The manufacturer's warranty for the watch is 1 year (12 months). Assume normal distribution.

43) What is the probability that the watch will break down within the warranty period and the manufacturer must cover the cost of repair?

A. 0.0031
B. 0.0122

C. 0.5739
D. 0.7287

44) What is the probability the watch will function for 25 months or longer?

A. 0.6917
B. 0.3085
C. 0.2660
D. 0.1288

45) To be more customer-friendly, the manufacturer has decided to change its warranty policy so the probability of service while under warranty is 0.03 or less. How many months should be set as the warranty period? Round up your answer to the nearest integer.

A. 13
B. 14
C. 15
D. 16

**Use the following information to answer Questions 46-47.**
The HR department of a local company administers a litmus test to applicants. The mean score on the test is 245 with a standard deviation equal to 28 points. Assume normal distribution.

46) What is the probability that an applicant scores between 230 and 280 points?

A. 0.6428
B. 0.7715
C. 0.8329
D. 0.5983

47) The manager wants to consider only those applicants who have scored in the **top 5%**. What score marks that cut-off point?

A. 291
B. 220
C. 199
D. 278

**Use the following information to answer Questions 48 – 50.**
The time between failures for an industrial machine is exponentially distributed with a mean of 37 days.

48) What is the probability that a failure occurs in the next 30 days?

A. 0.1288
B. 0.4469
C. 0.5555

D. 0.7253

49) What is the probability that a failure occurs in the next 20 to 50 days?

A. 0.1438
B. 0.3659
C. 0.2271
D. 0.3235

50) What is the probability that it will be 65 days or longer before the machine breaks down?

A. 0.0925
B. 0.1726
C. 0.4364
D. 0.5002

# Midterm Examination

The following problems need to be solved at home. I am assuming that you understand that these are open-book open-note, etc. since you are not being timed or supervised to solve these. You are welcome to solve these using MS Excel or by hand.

Remember to upload this portion as an attachment to the Assignment Tab in BlackBoard before 11:59PM on 09/17/2017. All work is expected to be done by yourself and late submissions are not acceptable.

This portion of the test is worth 30 points, and each of the following 2 questions are worth <u>15 points</u> EACH. Take your time, plan ahead, and start working on these problems to give yourself the time to get the best score possible for this attempt!

1. Employees of a local university have been classified according to gender and job type.

| | **Gender** | |
|---|---|---|
| **Job** | **Male (M)** | **Female (F)** |
| **Faculty Member (FA)** | 55 | 5 |
| **Salaried Staff (SS)** | 15 | 25 |
| **Hourly Staff (HS)** | 30 | 20 |

Calculate the following: (1.5 points each)

1) Complete the contingency table using Totals for rows and columns above.

2) If an employee is selected at random, what is the probability that the employee is male?

3) If an employee is selected at random, what is the probability that the employee is male and salaried staff?

4) If an employee is selected at random, what is the probability that the employee is female, given that the employee is a salaried member of the staff?

5) If an employee is selected at random, what is the probability that the employee is female or works as a member of the faculty?

6) If an employee is selected at random, what is the probability that the employee is female or works as an hourly staff member?

7) If an employee is selected at random, what is the probability that the employee is a member of the faculty?

8) If an employee is selected at random, what is the probability that the employee is a member of the hourly staff, given that the employee is female?

9) Are gender and type of job mutually exclusive?

10) Are gender and type of job statistically independent?

1. Suppose the probability that an individual has a particular medical condition is 0.10. Tests of an individual's

DNA can determine whether they have this medical condition but with only an 85 percent accuracy rate (that is, if the condition is present, the probability that the DNA test will give a positive finding is 0.85). If the medical condition is not present, the probability of the DNA test saying the medical condition exists is 0.03. What is the probability that the medical condition is present if the DNA test comes back positive?

www.ingramcontent.com/pod-product-compliance
Lightning Source LLC
LaVergne TN
LVHW082358200926
848481LV00012B/3609